FIRST GRAPHICS

WILD EARTH

VOLCANOES!

BY RENÉE GRAY-WILBURN

ILLUSTRATED BY ALEKSANDAR SOTIROVSKI

Consultant: Susan L. Cutter, PhD
Director, Hazards and Vulnerability Research Institute
Department of Geography
University of South Carolina, Columbia

CAPSTONE PRESS
a capstone imprint

First Graphics are published by Capstone Press,
1710 Roe Crest Drive, North Mankato, Minnesota 56003.
www.capstonepub.com

Library of Congress Cataloging-in-Publication Data
Gray-Wilburn, Renée.
  Volcanoes! / by Renée Gray-Wilburn ; illustrated by Aleksandar Sotirovski.
    p. cm.—(First graphics. Wild earth)
  Includes bibliographical references and index.
  Summary: "In graphic novel format, text and illustrations explain how
volcanoes erupt, how they are studied, and how to stay safe during an
eruption"—Provided by publisher.
  ISBN 978-1-4296-7606-9 (library binding)
  ISBN 978-1-4296-7953-4 (paperback)
  1. Volcanoes—Juvenile literature. I. Sotirovski, Aleksandar, ill. II. Title.
III. Series.
  QE521.3.G728 2012
  551.21—dc23   2011028742

Editorial Credits
Christopher Harbo, editor; Juliette Peters, designer;
    Nathan Gassman, art director; Kathy McColley,
    production specialist

Printed in the United States of America in North Mankato, Minnesota.
042012   006696

Table of Contents

What Are Volcanoes?

A mountain stands high above a quiet forest.

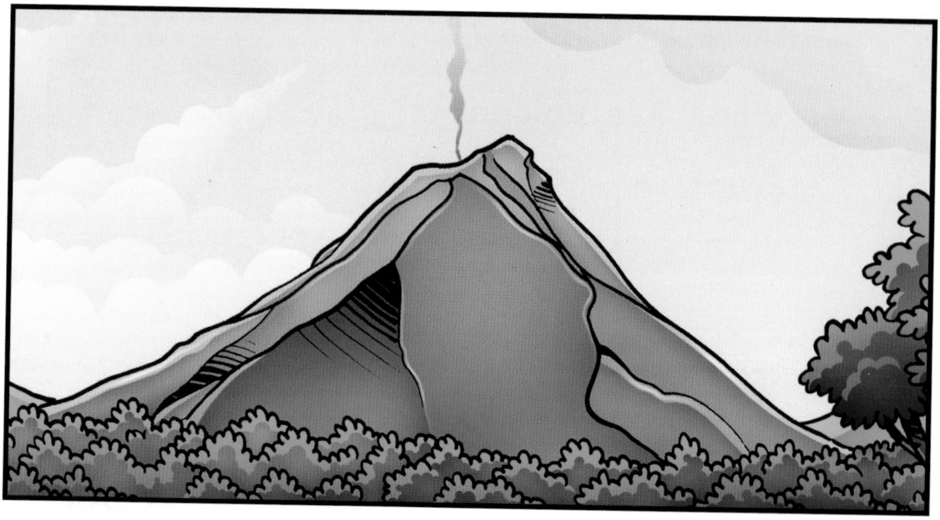

Suddenly, dark clouds of ash blast from its top.

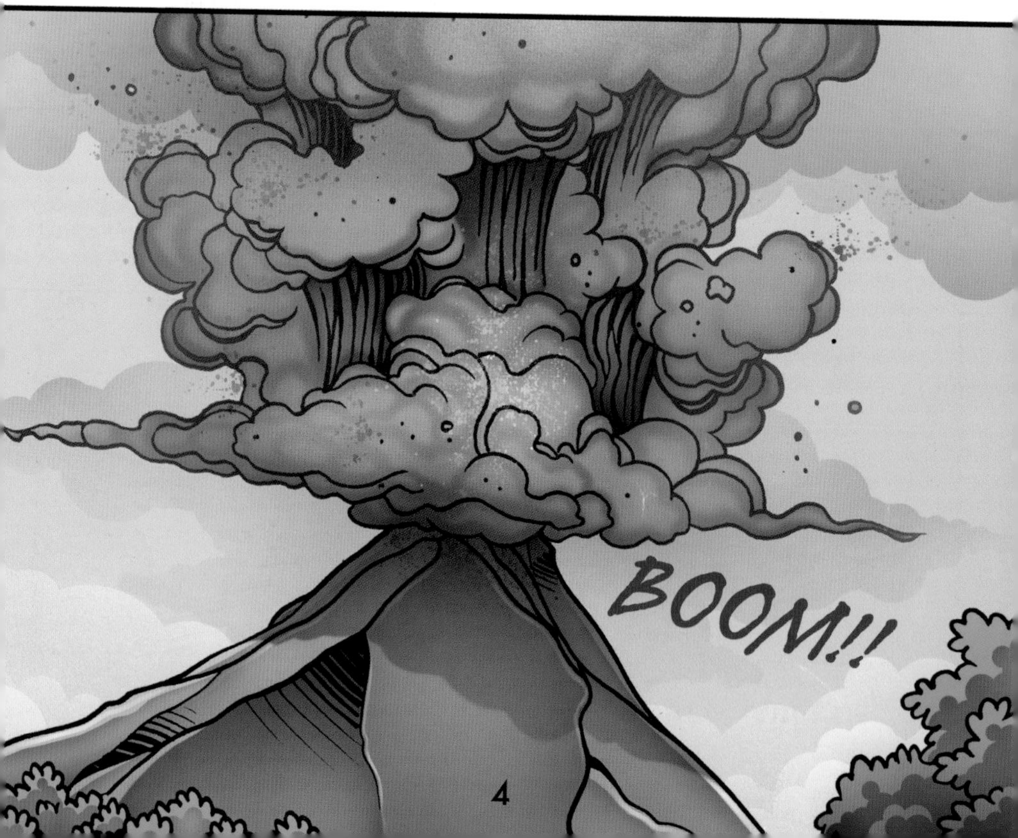
BOOM!!

Glowing orange lava pours down its sides.

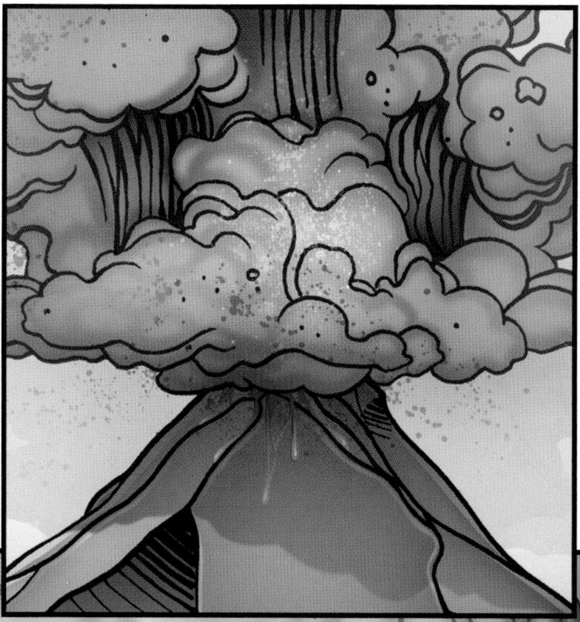

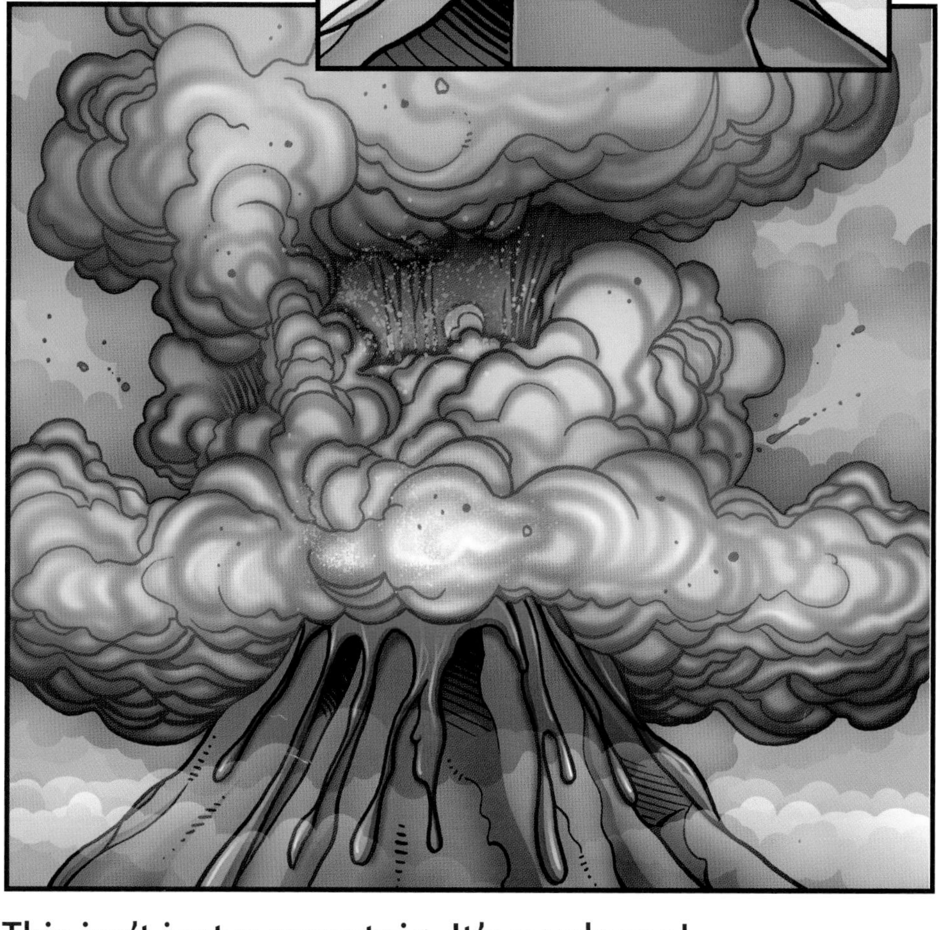

This isn't just a mountain. It's a volcano!

A volcano forms when an opening in Earth's surface pushes out lava and gases.

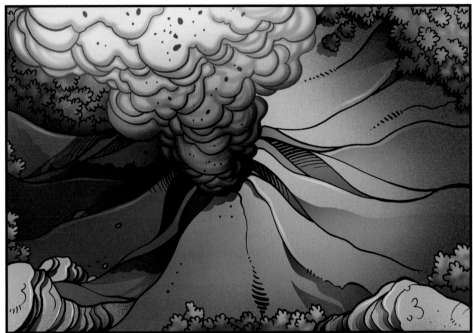

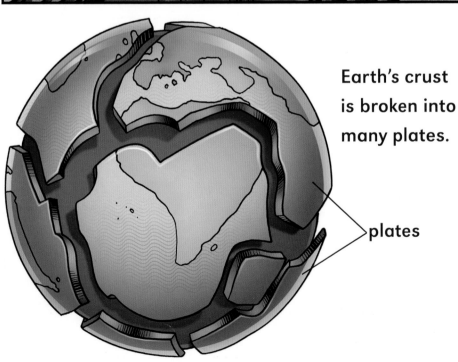

Earth's crust is broken into many plates.

plates

As plates move, melted rock called magma sometimes rises between them. When magma reaches the surface, its called lava.

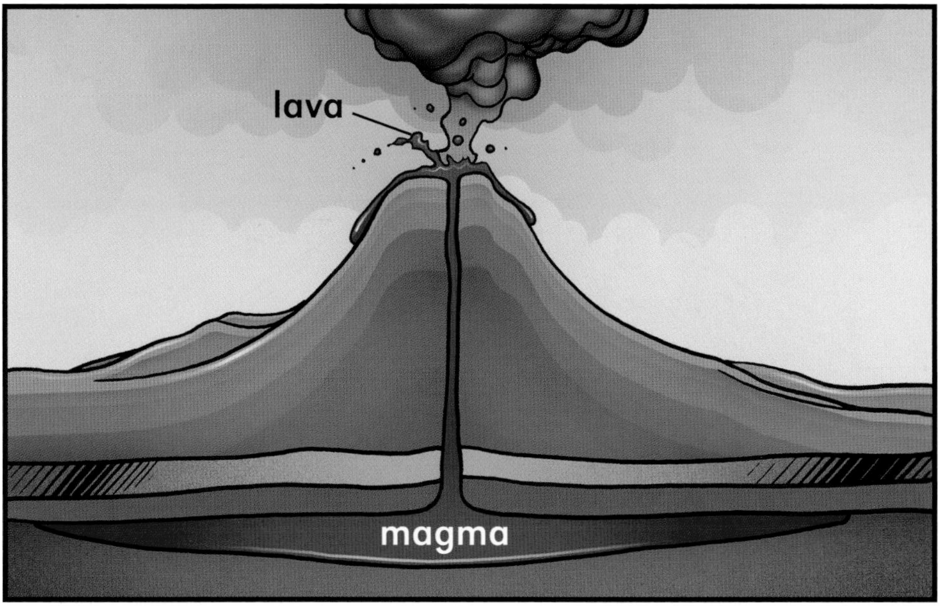
lava
magma

Most volcanoes are found near the Pacific Ocean. This area is called the Ring of Fire.

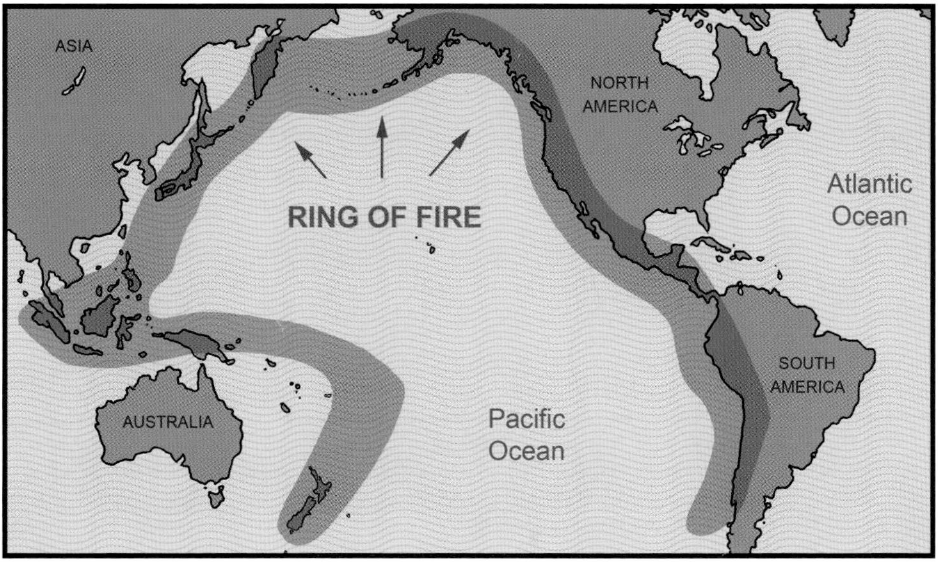
ASIA
NORTH AMERICA
RING OF FIRE
Atlantic Ocean
SOUTH AMERICA
AUSTRALIA
Pacific Ocean

Volcanoes have many shapes and sizes.
Some look like tall, steep cones.

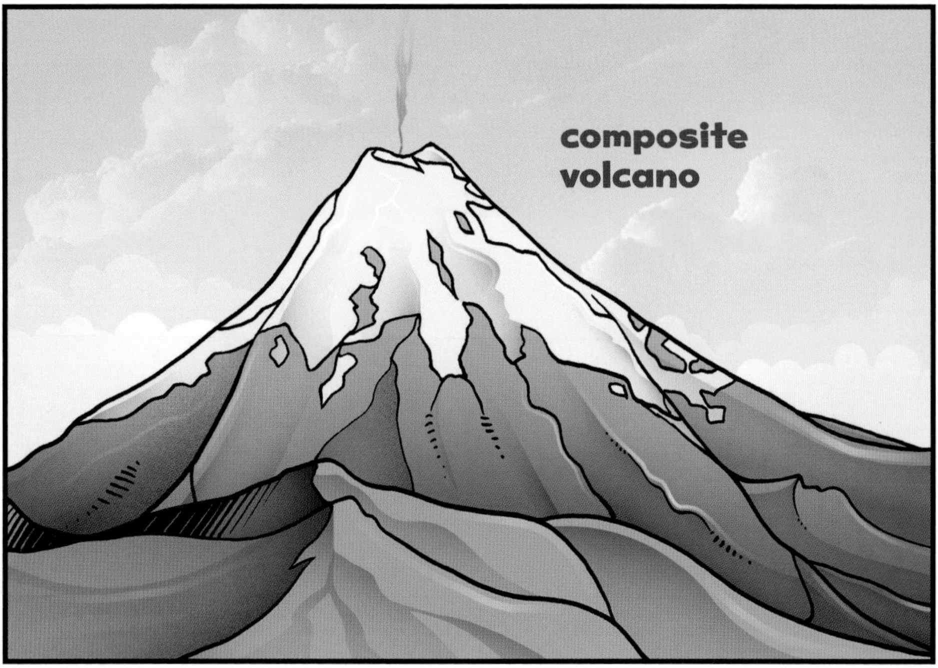
composite
volcano

Others are short, round, and wide.

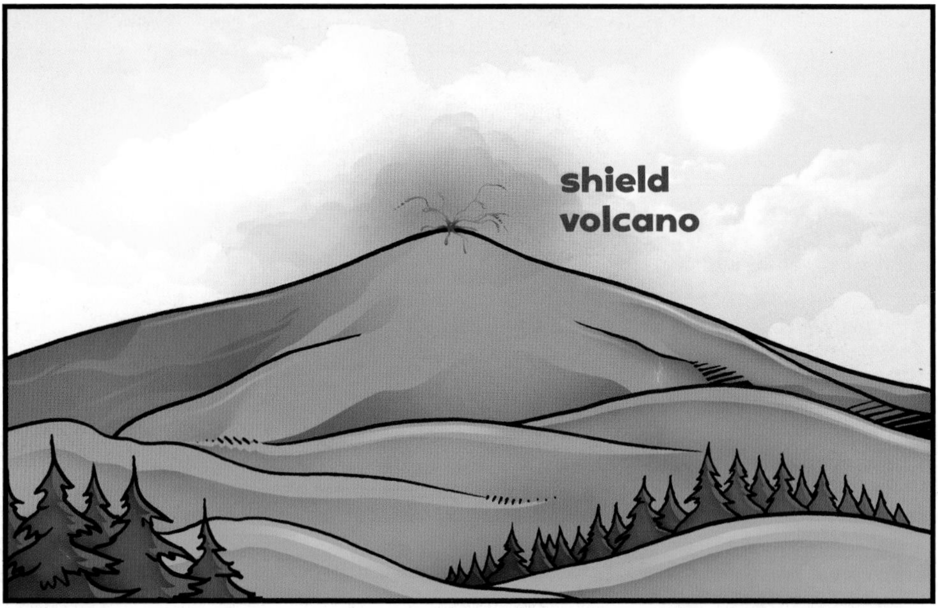
shield
volcano

Some volcanoes don't have cone shapes at all. They look like bowls.

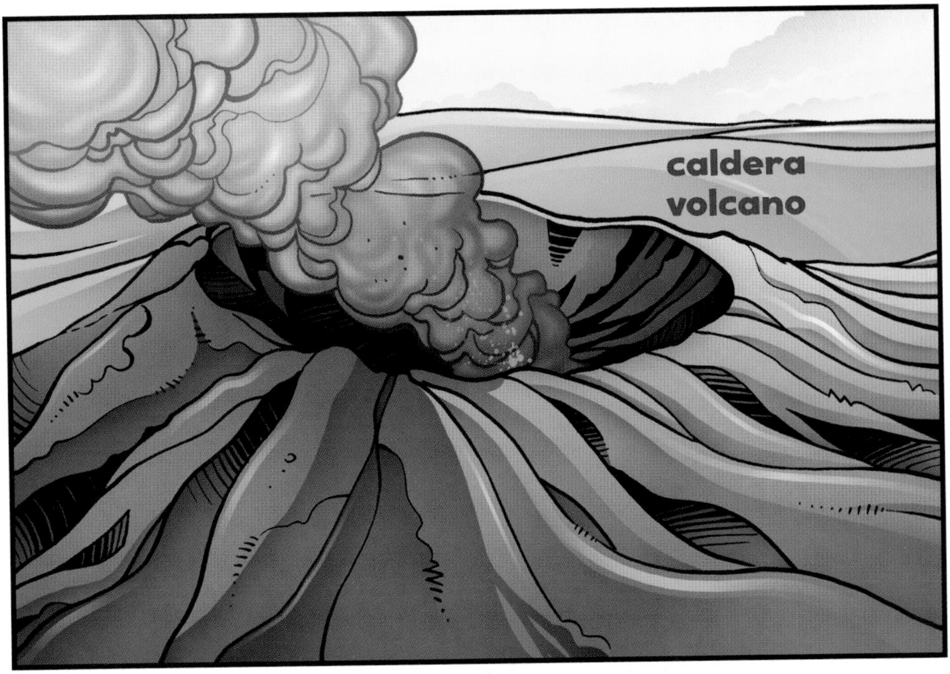
caldera
volcano

Underwater volcanoes sometimes become islands.

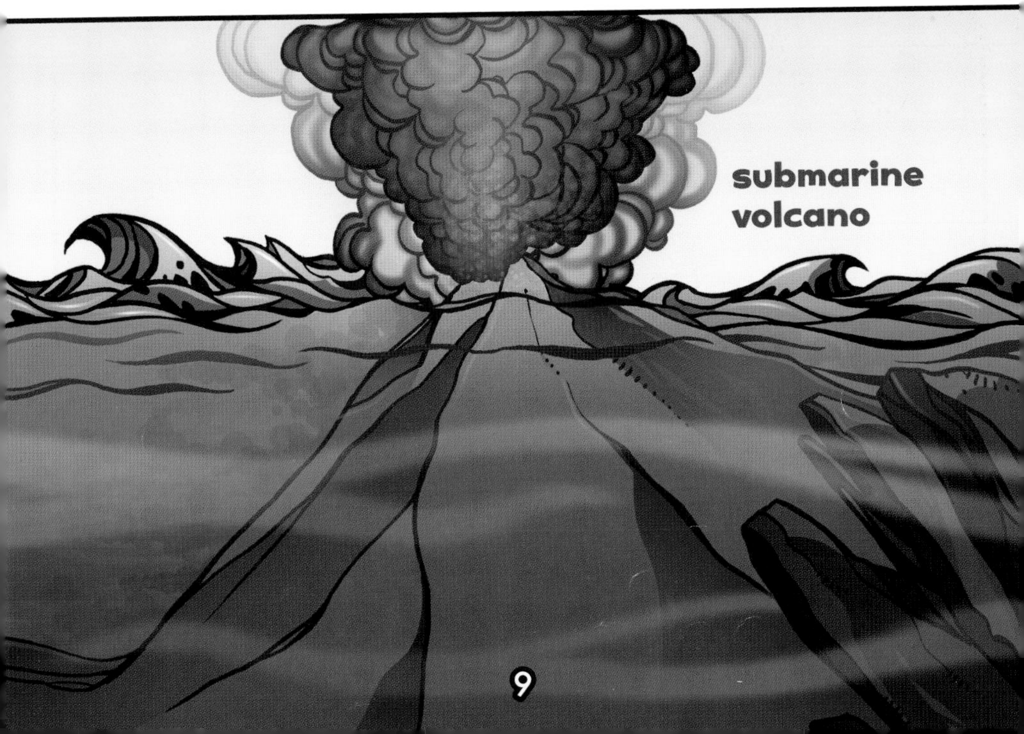
submarine
volcano

Eruption!

A volcano erupts when pressure builds deep inside Earth. Magma is pushed toward the surface.

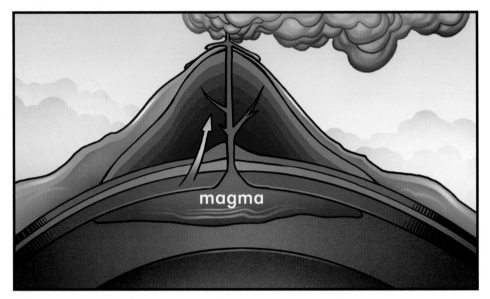

The magma rises through the volcano's center. It bursts from the volcano's top.

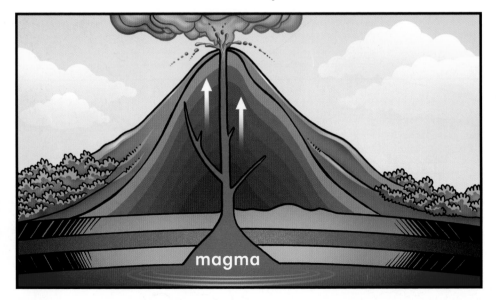

Lava flows down the volcano's sides. Hot ash and gases rise from the top.

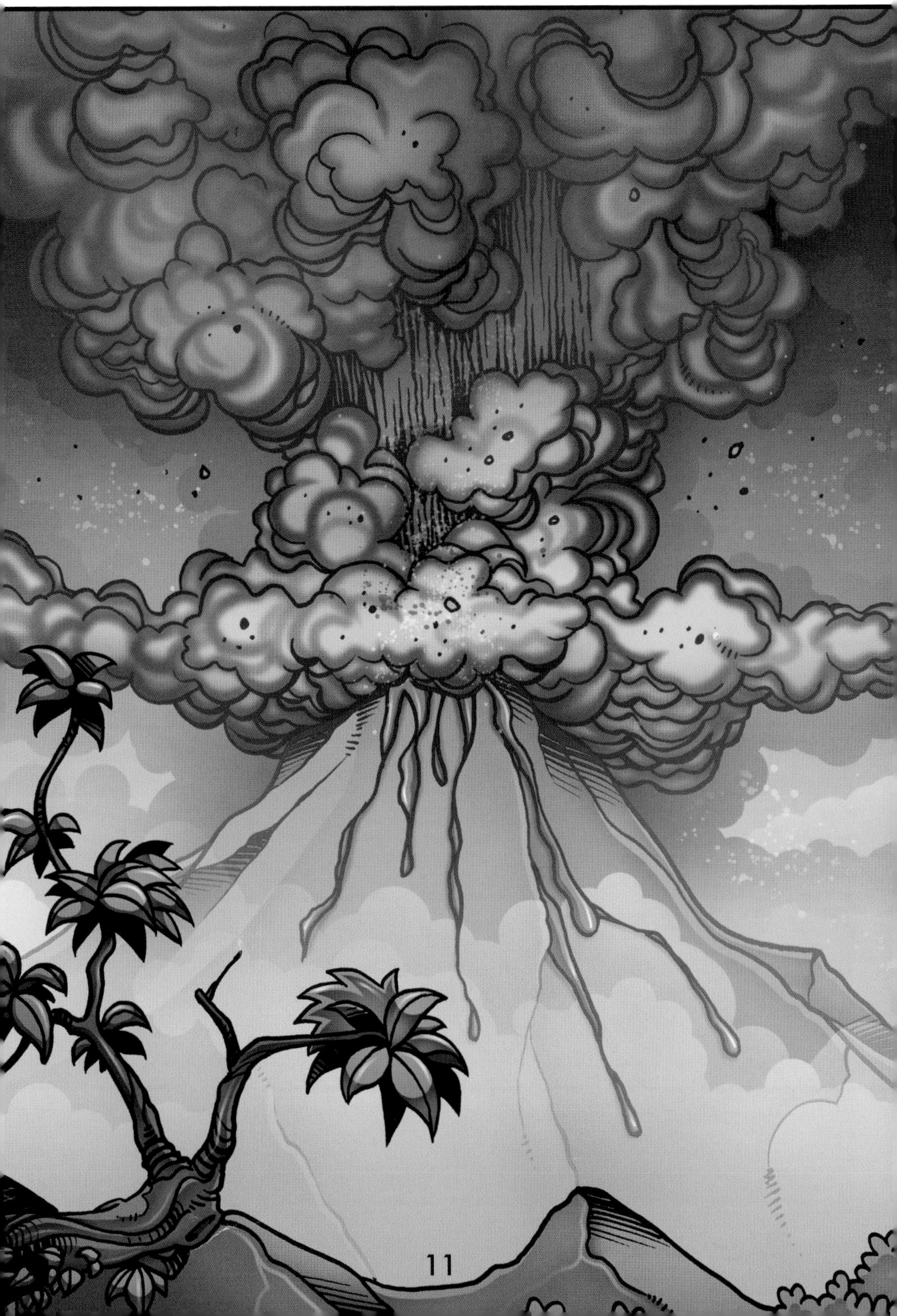

Sometimes lava flows slowly down the volcano.

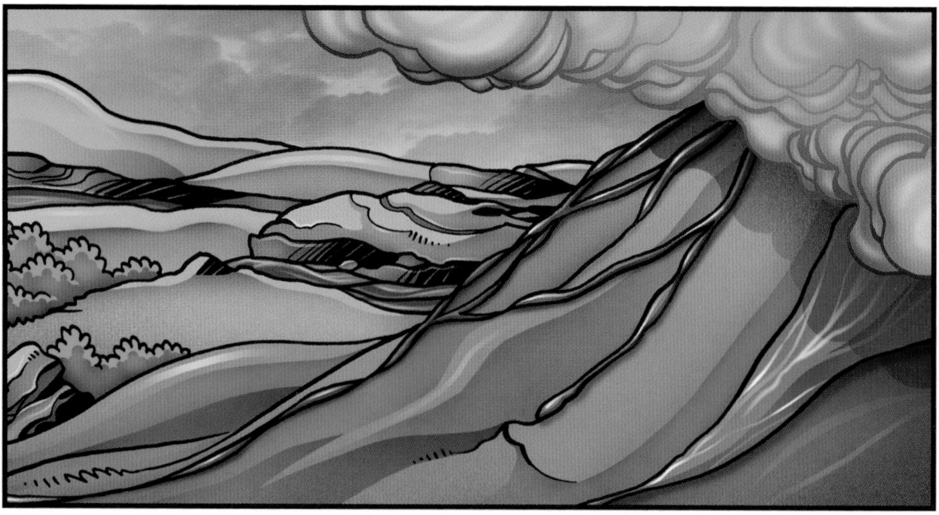

Other times, it explodes out of the volcano.

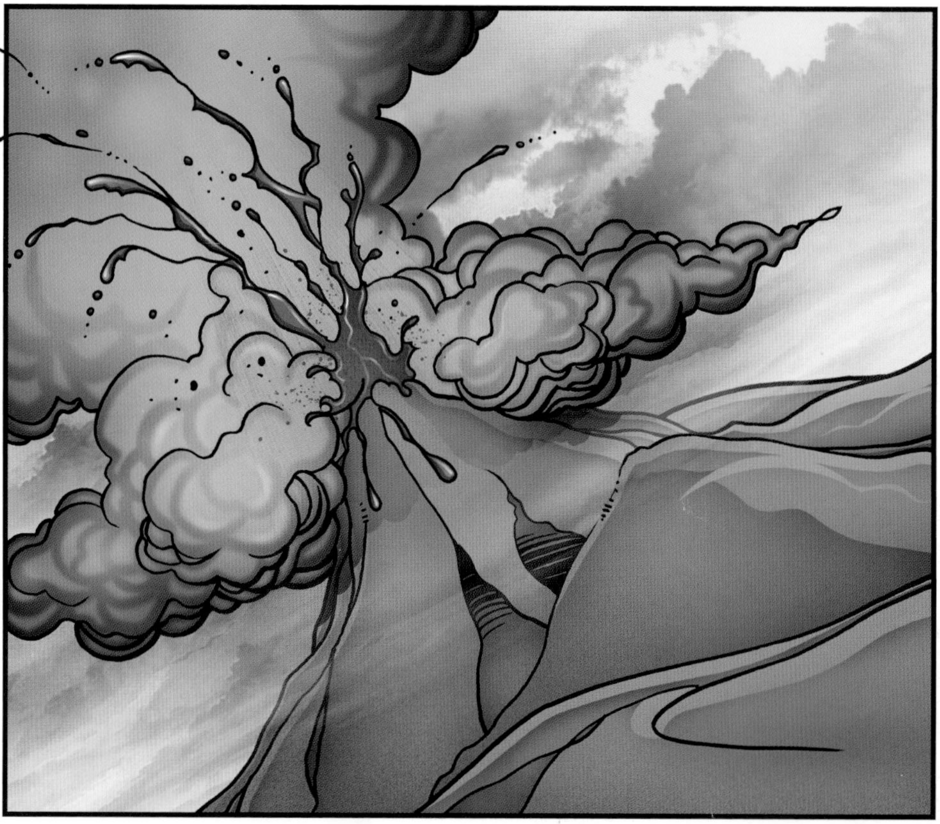

Over time, the lava cools and hardens into rock.

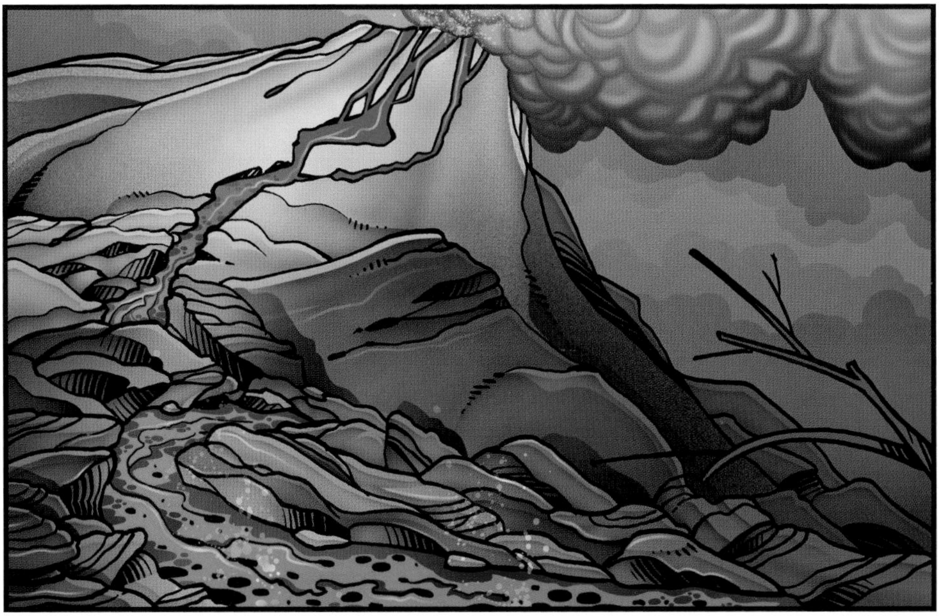

This hard rock builds up in layers. The volcano grows taller and wider.

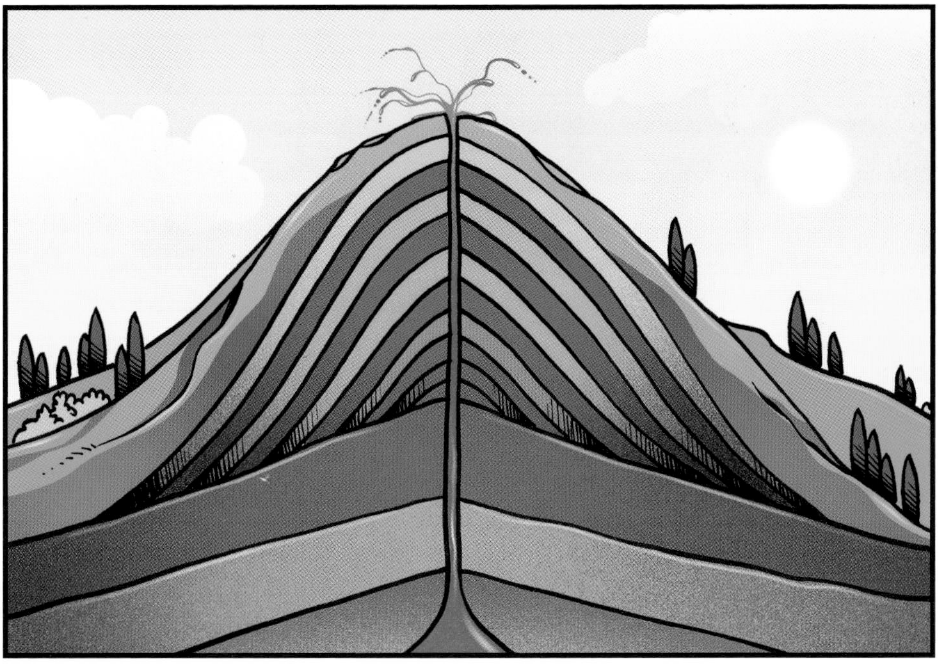

A volcano's ash and gases are harmful.

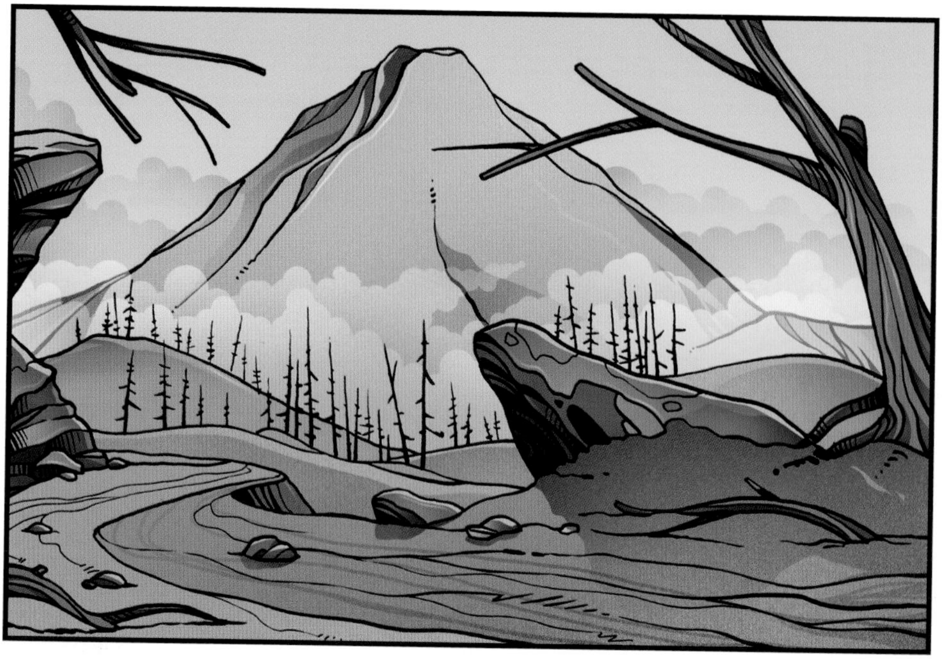

Ash mixes with steam to make thick mud.
This mud flows down volcanoes.

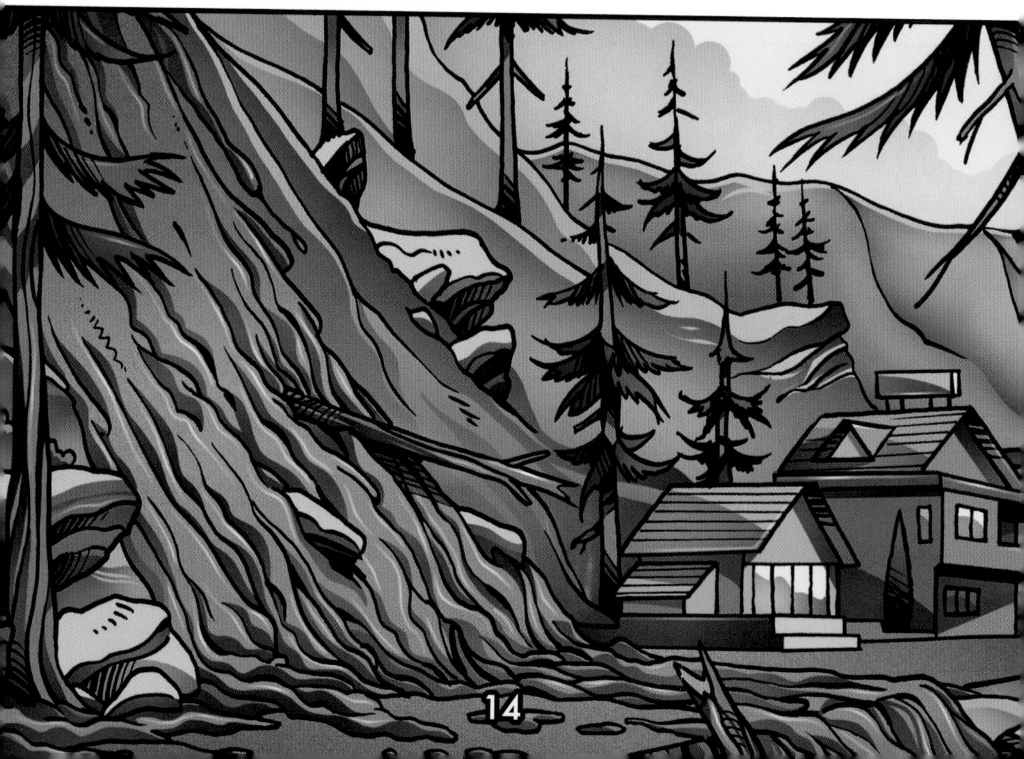

Huge clouds of hot gases and ash burn everything in their path.

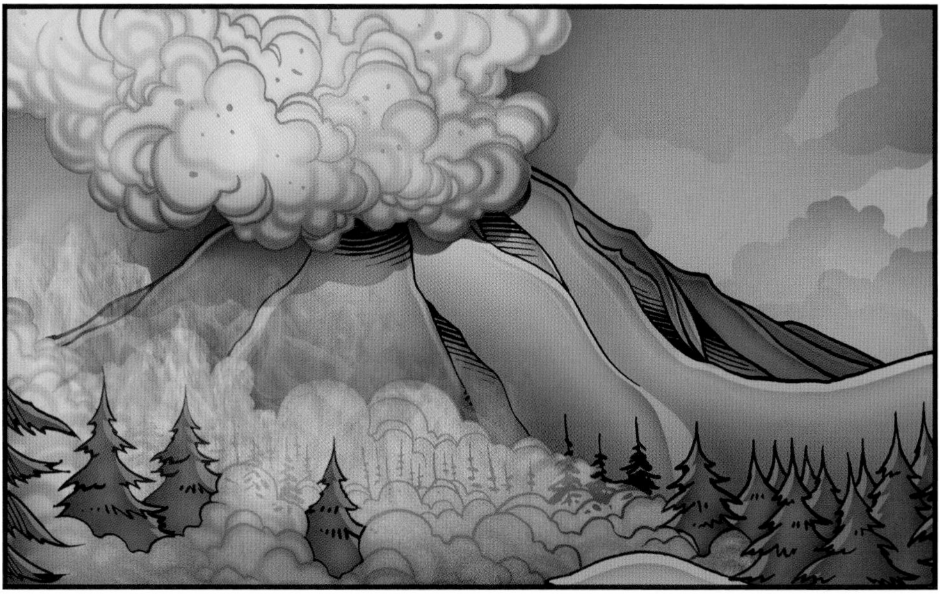

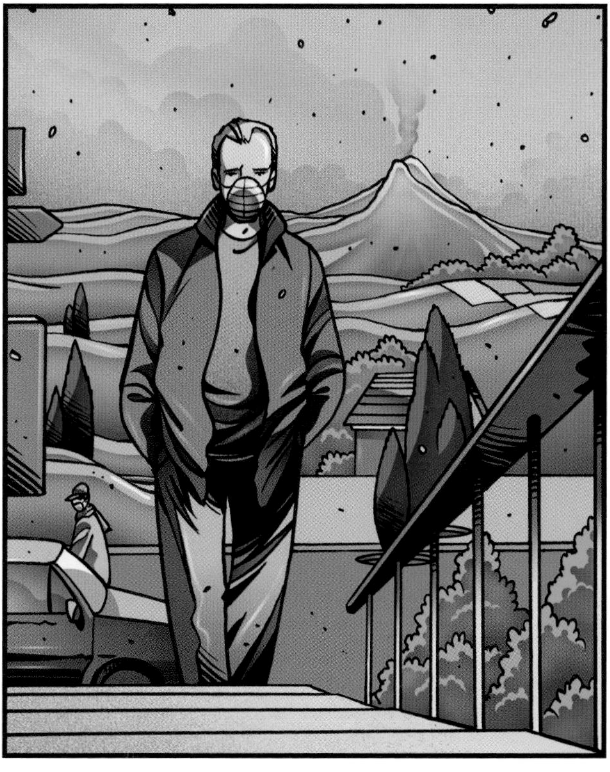

The ash and gases aren't safe to breathe.

Be Prepared

Scientists study volcanoes to learn more about them.

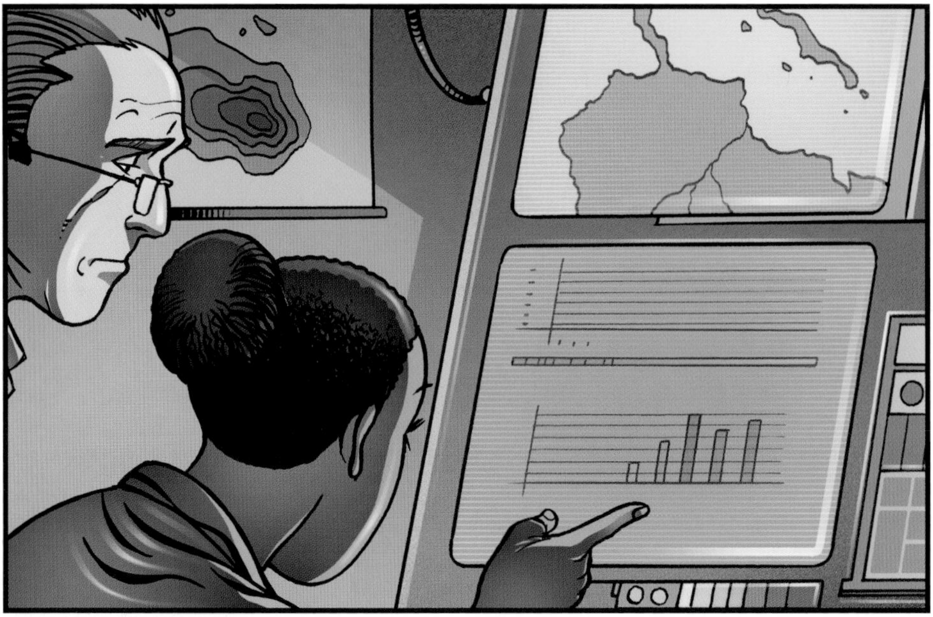

They test the temperature of lava.

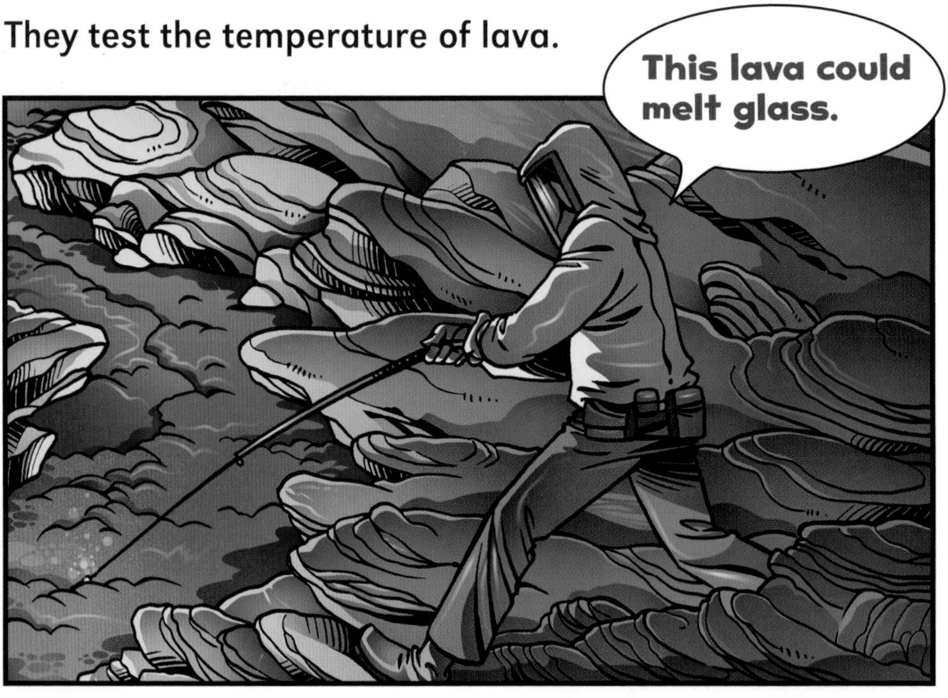
This lava could melt glass.

They measure the types of gases coming out of a volcano.

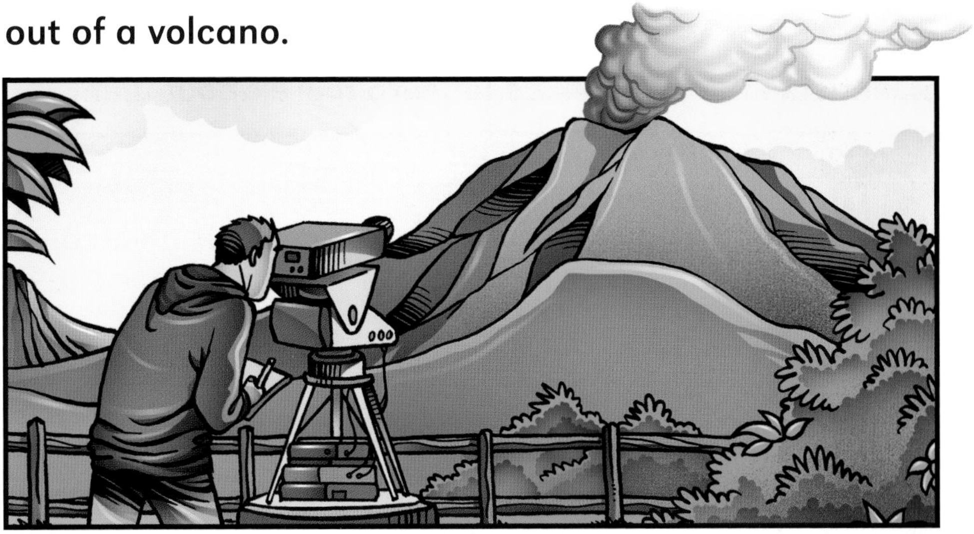

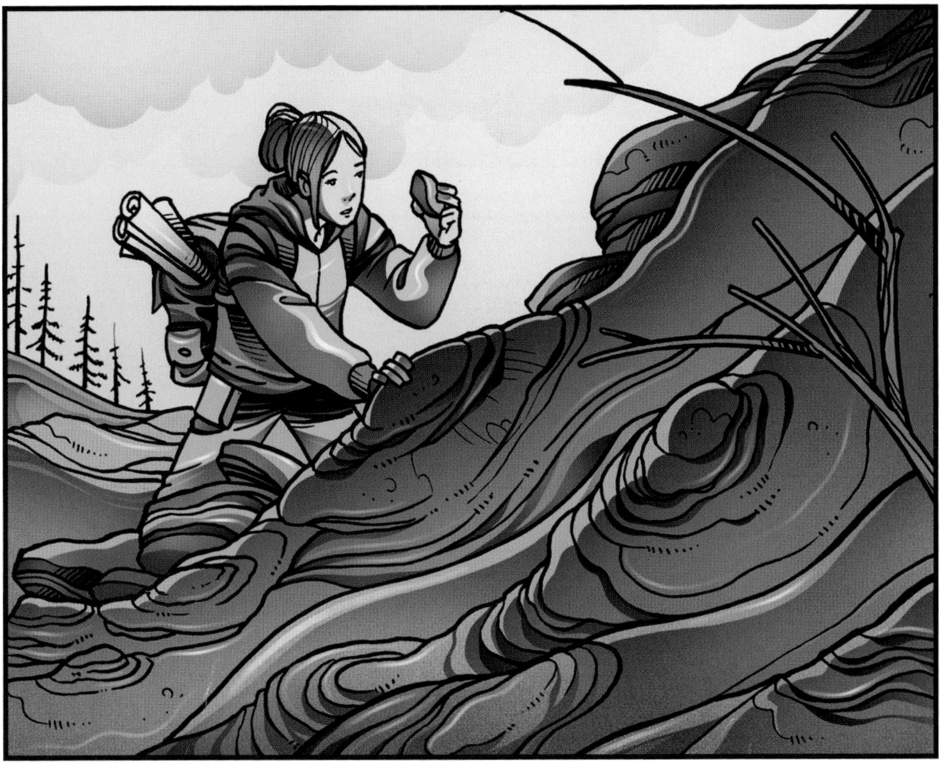

They study layers of hardened lava to understand a volcano's history.

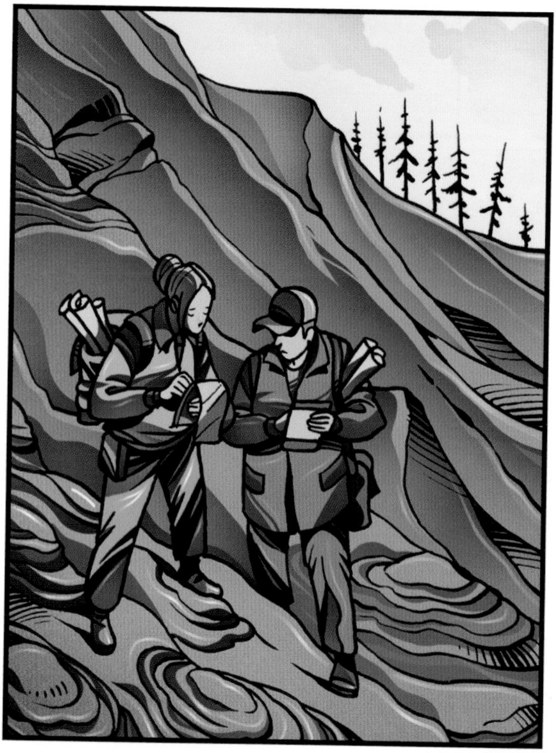

Scientists watch for signs that a volcano will erupt.

Rising lava can cause earthquakes inside the volcano.

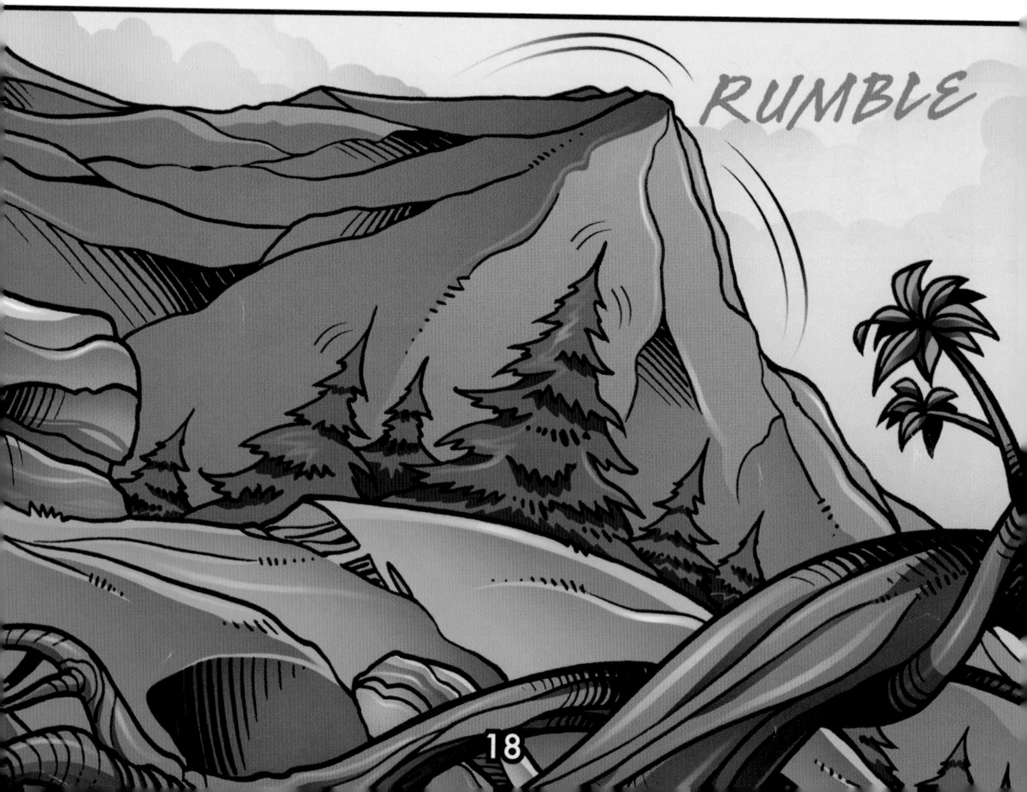
RUMBLE

Rock and ash can shoot out of a volcano.

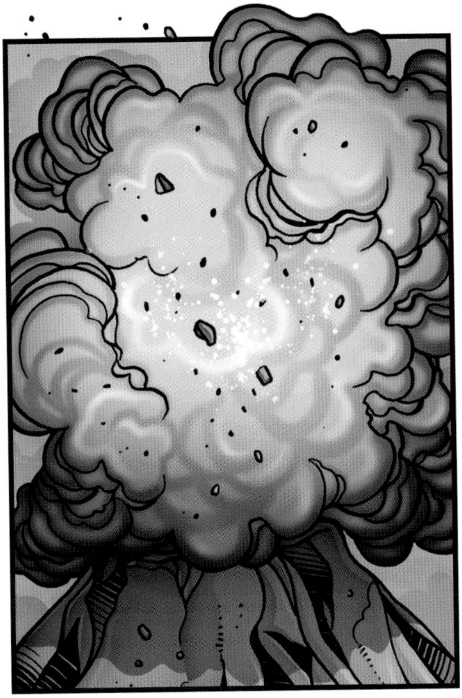

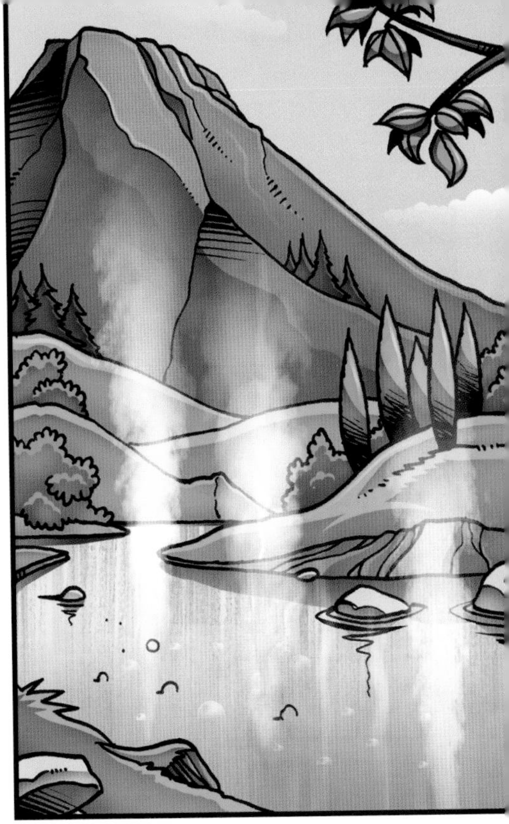

Sometimes nearby rivers and lakes heat up.

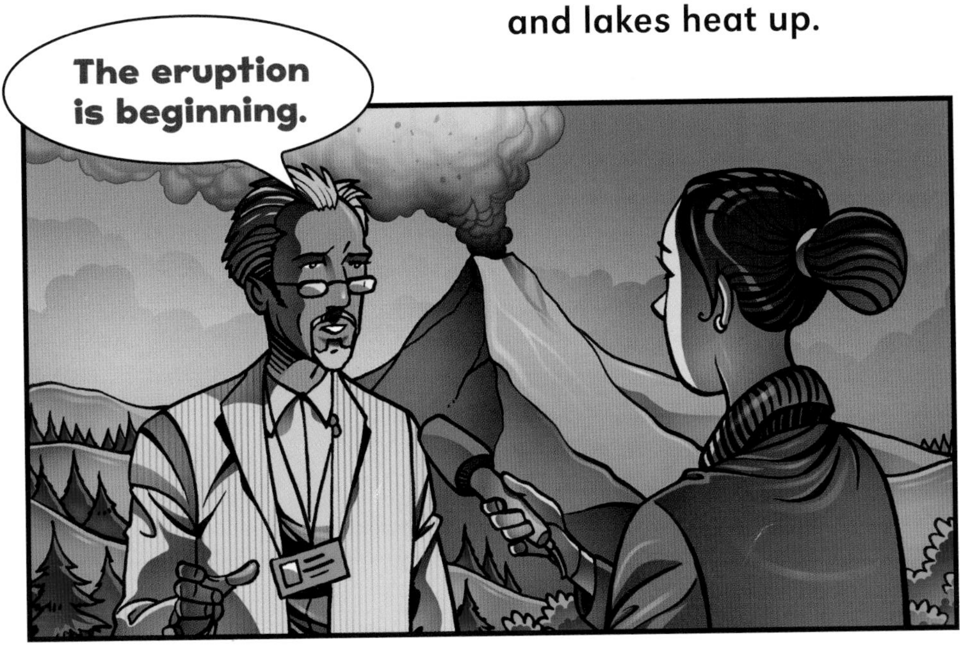
The eruption is beginning.

These clues help scientists warn people.

Most volcanoes erupt slowly. People living near them usually have enough time to leave the area.

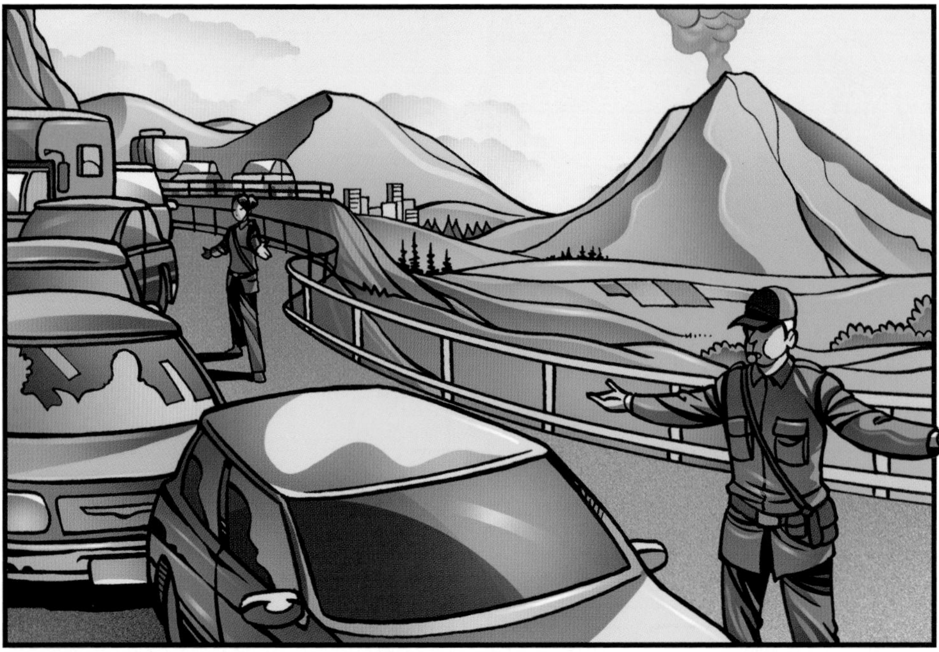

Always have an emergency plan and supply kit ready.

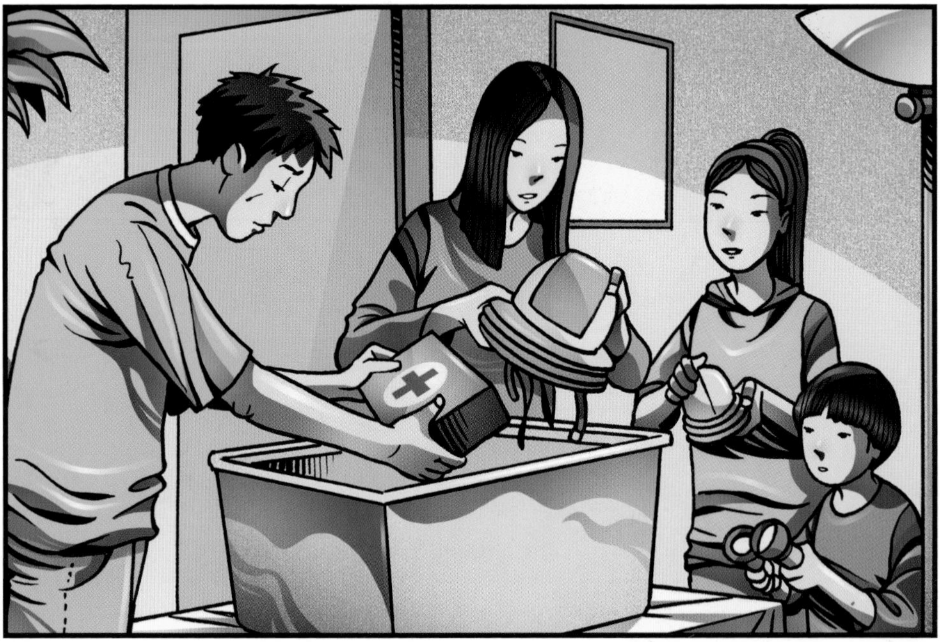

Go to a safe place away from the volcano.

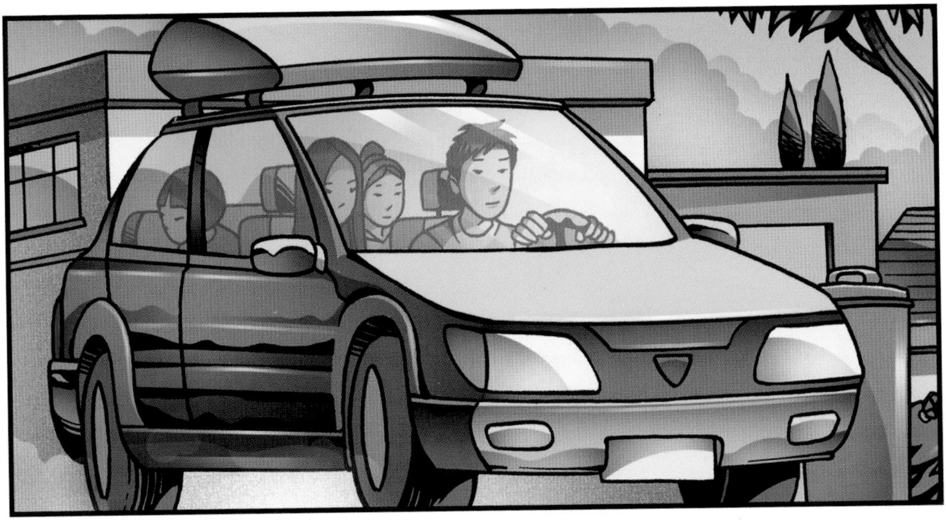

Knowing what to do when a volcano erupts will help keep you safe.

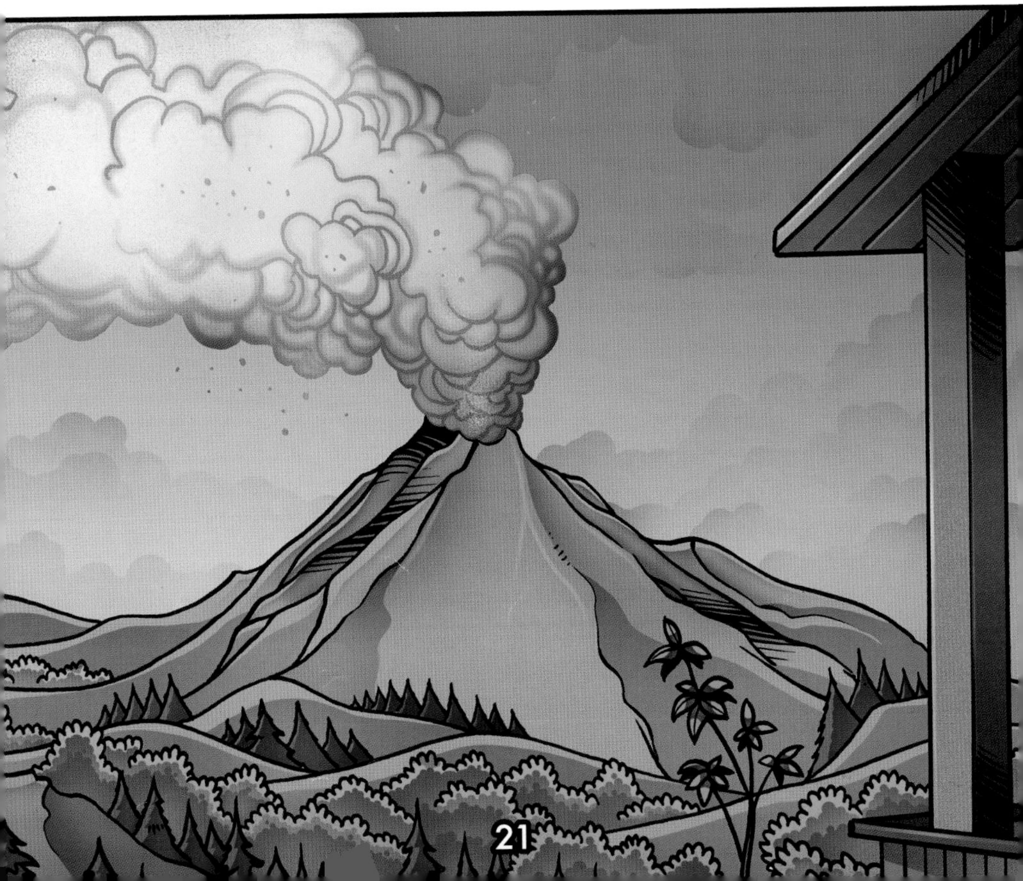

Glossary

ash—a powder that results from an explosion; ash comes out of a volcano when it erupts

crust—the hard outer layer of Earth

erupt—to burst out suddenly with great force

lava—the hot, liquid rock that pours out of a volcano when it erupts

magma—melted rock that is found beneath Earth's crust

plate—a large sheet of rock that is a piece of Earth's crust

pressure—the force produced by pressing on something

Read More

Mara, Wil. *Why Do Volcanoes Erupt?* Tell Me Why, Tell Me How. Tarrytown, N.Y.: Marshall Cavendish Benchmark, 2010.

Nault, Jennifer. *Volcanoes.* Earth Science. New York: AV2 by Weigl, 2010.

Schuh, Mari. *Volcanoes.* Earth in Action. Mankato, Minn.: Capstone Press, 2010.

Internet Sites

FactHound offers a safe, fun way to find Internet sites related to this book. All of the sites on FactHound have been researched by our staff.

Here's all you do:

Visit *www.facthound.com*

Type in this code: 9781429676069

Check out projects, games and lots more at
www.capstonekids.com

Index

WILD EARTH

Titles in this Set:

EARTHQUAKES!
HURRICANES!
TORNADOES!
VOLCANOES!

FIRST GRAPHICS